THE POCKET GUIDE TO

OLD-TIME CATFISH

TECHNIQUES

THE POCKET GUIDE TO
OLD-TIME
CATFISH
TECHNIQUES

AN ANGLER'S QUICK REFERENCE BOOK

MONTE BURCH

Skyhorse Publishing

Skyhorse Publishing books may be purchased in bulk at special discounts for sales promotion, corporate gifts, fund-raising, or educational purposes. Special editions can also be created to specifications. For details, contact the Special Sales Department, Skyhorse Publishing, 307 West 36th Street, 11th Floor, New York, NY 10018 or info@skyhorsepublishing.com.

Skyhorse® and Skyhorse Publishing® are registered trademarks of Skyhorse Publishing, Inc.®, a Delaware corporation.

Visit our website at www.skyhorsepublishing.com.

10 9 8 7 6 5 4 3 2

Library of Congress Cataloging-in-Publication Data is available on file.

Cover design by Tom Lau
Cover image credit: iStockphoto.com/Vasiliy Voropaev

Print ISBN: 978-1-63450-811-7
Ebook ISBN: 978-1-63450-820-9

Printed in China

CONTENTS

INTRODUCTION

Catfishing on a slow, central Missouri river was my dad's passion. I still remember those nights, listening to the whistle of the camp lantern and waiting for the jerk of the metal rod at the bite of an unseen cat. The old river is gone, buried beneath a sprawling reservoir, but the catfish are there, in even bigger numbers, and catching them on a dark summer night has the same mystery and excitement.

Catfishing is a favorite pastime of many anglers; in fact, catfish are second only to bass in popularity. Over two thousand species of cats exist worldwide, but the most common and favored of American anglers include the bullheads, blue cat, white cat, flathead, and channel cat.

Catfishing is one of the most enjoyable, relaxing, yet exciting forms of freshwater angling in North America. Catfishing can be enjoyed by the entire family and without a lot of fancy equipment. In fact, you don't even have to own a boat for some of the best in catfishing. Catfishing also offers the chance at not only some great eating, but exciting catching, especially when you grab ahold of a monster blue or flathead catfish.

Catfishing can be simple or technical, using the old-time secrets as well as a few new ideas illustrated in this book on all types of catfishing.

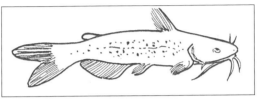

Channel Cat

Channel Cat

The single most popular catfish across America is the channel cat. First is their great taste. They're also easily propagated and stocked in farm ponds, rivers, streams, and lakes, providing great sport fishing as well as an entire industry selling live or dressed fish. They're found almost everywhere. Adults will range in length from 20 to 44 inches and weigh from 3 to 40 pounds. They can, however, get huge. The record is a 58-pound monster caught from the Santee Cooper Reservoir in July of 1964.

Their native range includes the central drainages of the United States and Canada, as well as some parts of the Atlantic coast. Because of their ease of propagation and popularity, they have been introduced throughout the United States and much of northern Mexico.

Because of the introduction into different waters, channel cats are found in a wide variety of habitat ranging from farm ponds to lakes, reservoirs, and large and small streams. In their natural range, channel cats prefer large to medium streams with medium gradient, and some current, spending the majority of their time in deeper holes with lots of cover such as submerged logs and log jams.

Most of the daylight hours are spent in the deeper holes near or in cover. At night the channel cat comes out to roam and feed. Primarily bottom feeders, channel cats will take almost anything from live food such as fish, crawfish, and mollusks to plant materials. Feeding primarily by taste rather than sight, they'll also readily take other materials and have been known to exist in large numbers below the outflow of slaughter and rendering houses on rivers.

Channel cats spawn in natural cavities, including muskrat dens, under undercut banks, and so forth, in a nest cleaned out by the male. Normal spawning temperature is 60 to 65 degrees. In ponds and lakes where catfish are managed, barrels or concrete "tiles" are used to provide nesting sites. The females don't participate in the nest building or protection of the eggs. The male guards the nest until the fry leave.

Channel cats are caught using everything from trotlines, jug lines, and limb lines to rods and reels, and on baits ranging from commercially prepared baits to hot dogs. Any number of home-brewed or manufactured baits using cheese, chicken entrails, gizzards, and blood as well as other secret ingredients are used to entice channel cats.

Channel cats can become wary of a baited hook. The best rig utilizes a sliding egg sinker so the cat won't feel the weight on line when it takes the bait. One unusual and exciting method is to use spinners, small spoons, and other artificial baits fished slowly along the bottom. This is especially effective over riffles at night. At night or near dusk is the single best time to fish for channel cats. Another excellent time is after a heavy rain when the river is rising.

Bullheads

Lowest on the catfish "social scale" is the common bullhead with three species: the

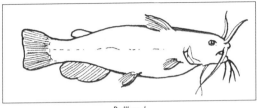

Bullhead

Black Bullhead (*Ictalurus melas*), the Brown
Bullhead (*Ictalurus nebulosus*), and the
Yellow Bullhead (*Ictalurus natalis*). These
were my first fish, caught from a muddy
cattle watering pond on my dad's place,
beginning before I even went to school.

The black bullhead, also called a mud cat
or horned pout, is a short, chunky catfish,
evenly colored black, dark olive or yellowish brown on back and sides with a pale
vertical bar across the base of the tail fin.
(This doesn't exist on other bullheads.)
The belly is white or yellow. The record
is a 6-pound-2-ounce fish caught from the
Pearl River in Mississippi in January of 1991.

The yellow bullhead is uniformly yellow to yellow-brown on the back and sides with a white to light yellow belly. The yellow bullhead record is 4 pounds, 8 ounces, from Mormon Lake, Arizona, in July of 1989.

Although the natural range of all three bullheads is primarily the eastern half of the United States, they have been widely transplanted and are now found in almost all of the lower forty-eight states, with the black bullhead the most prevalent.

The habitat, habits, and life history of all three species is quite similar, with some variations on preferred habitat. All three are found in backwater sloughs, small, slow-moving creeks, muddy oxbows, ponds, and small lakes. They prefer quiet, turbid water with a silty bottom and little or no current. The permanent pools of tiny creeks are often a choice spot for black bullheads, while the yellow and brown bullheads prefer more submerged vegetation. The yellow bullhead, however, prefers clearer water than the other two and is found in small streams with permanent, but normally slow, current.

Immature aquatic insects and small crustaceans make up the diet of these bottom feeders. Saucer-shaped nests are usually found beneath objects such as logs, and are tended by one or both parents. The young leave the nest in a ball-like school, and the schools of tiny black fish are easily recognized as they move along the shoreline.

Bullheads provide angling pleasure for fishermen of all ages. They're eager biters and readily take prepared or live bait. The most successful tactic is also the simplest. A hook baited with a glob of earthworms with a split shot or two about 6 inches above the hook is tossed out and allowed to settle to the bottom. The rod is normally held in a bank rod holder and the slack removed from the line. Then wait until the tip of the rod dips when the catfish takes the bait. Most productive tactic is to let the cat nibble on the bait until he swallows it and there is a steady tug on the line. Just be patient. If small cats keep stealing the bait, you may have to set the hook a bit faster.

Blue Cat

The blue catfish (*Ictalurus furcatus*) is just the opposite of the diminutive bullhead. Adult blue cats commonly reach 44 inch-

Blue Cat

es in length and over 40 pounds. The official all-tackle record is 143 pounds from Buggs Island (John Kerr Reservoir) in North Carolina in July of 2011. A blue cat from the Osage River in central Missouri, near my home, weighed 117 pounds and was 5 feet, 3 inches long, but it is not entered in modern records because it was caught on a trotline many years ago.

The blue cat is bluish silver on the back and sides graduating to silver-white on the lower sides and belly. It has a distinct wedge-shaped body forward of the dorsal fin.

The native distribution of the blue cat is from Minnesota down through the Gulf Coast states, with the biggest distribution in the Mississippi River basin and its tributaries. The blue cat has been transplanted to some of the Atlantic coastal rivers as well.

Ol' Blue, as the Osage River giant was called, was typical of his species. Primarily a big river cat, they prefer the swift chutes and pools with current. With the advent of the locks, dams, and reservoirs created on many big rivers, the blue cat has also become a lake dweller. Numbers have declined in some areas greatly since the early 1900s when these giants, ranging up to 200 pounds, were often caught in rivers such as the Missouri and Mississippi. Their numbers in many reservoirs, however, are fairly high.

The blue cat, like most other catfish, will readily take many foods and is primarily a bottom feeder. They prefer, however, live fish, crawfish, mussels and aquatic insects in rivers, feeding in the swift-flowing chutes of stream bottoms. In reservoirs, and some rivers, their main food is shad, or similar forage.

Like most cats, blues build nests in sheltered areas under rocks, logs, ledges, and so forth, and both parents tend the nest.

The blue is a favorite because of its size, the fine flavor of its flesh, and the fish's fighting ability. Trotlines are a favorite tactic in both rivers and reservoirs. Jug fishing is another popular and productive tactic.

A large plastic jug or "noodle" with a weighted line and hook baited with a chunk of meat, cut bait or fresh bait is drifted down the river, or set loose on a reservoir. The most exciting tactic, however, is rod and reel fishing the tailrace water below dams. During certain times of the year, blues congregate in big numbers in these areas. The size of the fish, combined with the heavy current, provides lots of fresh-water, big-game action. Many tailraces have off-limits areas below the dam for boaters or bank anglers, and are also too large to effectively cast from the bank to the midstream areas. Anglers use big, 12-foot surf rods to cast the distance and battle big fish.

One tactic in reservoirs is to drift fish the flats. This can also result in some mighty big cats. Make sure you follow local rules regarding the number of hooks or rods.

White Catfish

The white cat (*Ictalurus catus*) is similar to the blue cat, except it doesn't get quite as large and is found primarily in the east. Their normal range is from Pennsylvania down to the gulf coast.

Flathead Catfish

With a lower jaw protruding like a pit bull, and a body like a sumo wrestler,

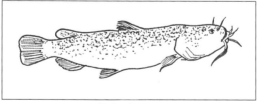

Flathead

only a mother could like a flathead catfish (*Pylodictis olivaris*)—and the legions of anglers who readily pursue this popular catfish. The general coloration of the flathead is yellowish brown mottled with darker brown. The edges of the caudal fin are lighter than the rest of the fin, often yellow or white. The flathead has a large "flat" head and a rounded instead of forked tail. Although the size ranges from a couple to 45 pounds, and the length from 15 to 45 inches, flatheads can often reach over 100 pounds. The official record is 123 pounds, taken from Elk City Reservoir, in Oklahoma in May of 1998.

Found primarily in the larger river systems from Minnesota and the Great Lakes south to the Gulf, the flathead catfish has been introduced to some areas outside its native range as well.

Like the blue, the flathead prefers the bigger and medium-sized rivers, although they have done extremely well in the reservoirs created on many of these rivers. They prefer the deeper, quieter holes on these rivers; however, younger cats will often be found around riffles.

Flatheads are predators and prefer live food. Older cats often feed at night, moving from their deep water, daytime haunts to the riffles and stream banks to feed. Smaller flatheads take aquatic insects while the larger cats feed primarily on fish and crayfish. They rarely take dead or decaying matter and are not susceptible to the many "stink" baits. Flatheads spawn in a saucer-shaped bowl excavated in a large cavity, such as under a ledge, in a cave, and so forth. Both parents guard the nest containing a mass of golden-colored eggs. The parents continually fin the nest to keep silt from depositing on the eggs until they hatch. Within its range, the flathead is one of the most popular fish. Flatheads are big, taste great, and are readily caught on live bait. Trotlines or limb lines baited with perch, bluegill (where legal), and other live bait is the most popular method of catching flatheads.

Rod and reel fishing the riffles on rivers at night with live bait is also a popular and extremely exciting tactic for taking these big bruisers.

ROD & REEL FISHING

The most common method of catfishing is relaxing on a river, lake, or pond bank with a baited rod or two. Although this can be done almost any time and any place, it's most effective when cats are relatively shallow in lakes and ponds and during rising water on streams.

Regardless of the time of the year, when there is a rise in the river due to rain, the increase in current brings on a feeding binge in cats. This, however, normally occurs in spring and early summer and provides some of the best and most exciting catfish angling. The upper ends of the river systems are usually the best. Tributaries or even small creeks that are flushed with rising water are extremely good spots, as are small run-off spots that are pouring water into the river. It's more a matter of timing than anything else. You simply have to be on the river on the rise, or just as it crests.

You can often get an indication of whether a river is rising, stable, or dropping by watching the debris coming down the river. Large amounts of debris accompanied by foam indicates a rising river.

Later in the year, as the weather gets warmer, the best spots are downstream in the mouths of the larger tributaries that lead into a larger river or a lake. Current is the most important factor during the summer months, regardless of whether fishing a river or lake. The deeper channels of the old river beds will usually still have some current in them even in reservoirs, and although the fishing will be "deep," it's one of the best areas.

Some of the best catfishing is during the nighttime.

Good catfishing can be enjoyed throughout the day in many areas, but for some really exciting action, try night cats. When the sun goes down, the really big cats such as flatheads go on the prowl, and even channel cats are more active in many areas at night.

What you catch depends on where you fish. A pond will result in bullheads and channels, while a major river may produce blues, channels, and flatheads. Reservoirs and lakes can harbor all species.

Almost any gear you happen to have can be used; however, the gear should be sturdy. A good rod and spinning, spincasting, or baitcasting reel will suffice. Probably the most common catfishing outfit is a spincasting reel on a medium rod, although larger specialized outfits are often used for some types of catfishing. Regardless of choice, the line should be heavy, or the drag should be set fairly light.

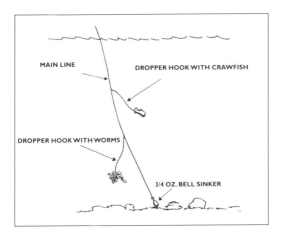

MAIN LINE

DROPPER HOOK WITH CRAWFISH

DROPPER HOOK WITH WORMS

3/4 OZ. BELL SINKER

You can't horse a big cat, especially from the bank with light line. You'll also need a good, heavy-duty net and something to hold your catch. An old burlap sack tied shut and immersed in the water was the traditional fish sack.

A typical bank rig consists of a ¾-ounce bell sinker tied on the end of 17- to 20-pound test main line. One or two dropper lines with 1/0 to 2/0 hooks are

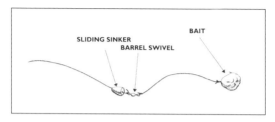

SLIDING SINKER

BARREL SWIVEL

BAIT

tied on the main line. Different types of baits on the hooks help determine the best bait choice.

Channel cats, however, can be wary and a rig using a sliding sinker is the best choice so they don't feel the weight.

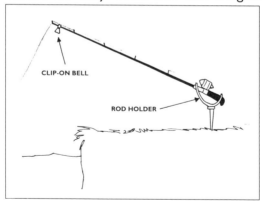

CLIP-ON BELL

ROD HOLDER

When the channel bites, let him take the line before setting the hook. A cone-shaped "worm" sinker can be used for less snagging.

Most serious catfishermen put out more than one rod (following local and state laws), then wait for the action to begin. The traditional old-fashioned rod holder is a forked stick pushed into the bank. Several modern rod holders are available, including some with built-in chairs. A tiny bell on the rod tip signals a bite. For night fishing, a lighted bobber can be used, or again a tiny bell mounted on the rod tip can signal a strike. A Coleman lantern placed between you and the rod tip can also help indicate strikes, and these days many rod manufacturers offer glow-in-the-dark rod tips. The technique is to gently lob the baited hooks out into the river or lake and place the rod in a holder. The slack in the line is taken up until the

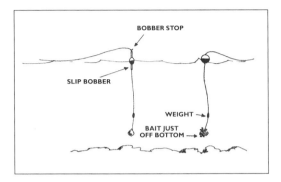

BOBBER STOP

SLIP BOBBER

WEIGHT →

BAIT JUST
OFF BOTTOM →

line is fairly "tight." A take by the cat will cause a jerk, or even slackening, of the line. In most instances cats will nibble a few times before they decide to take the bait. When the line starts going in the opposite direction, or the rod tip has a definite bow, grab ahold and start cranking.

BOBBER FISHING

Old-fashioned bobber fishing can also be productive. The bobber should be set so the bait is just off the bottom. Allow the wind to drift the bait or cast out and retrieve in slow jerks so the bait moves across the bottom. In deep water a slip bobber will help make long casts.

Many anglers fish for spawning cat-fish off the rocks in southern reservoirs. Man-made riprap areas like bridge approaches, causeways, marina or steam plant harbors, natural rock bluffs, broken shale banks that shelve off deeply—any of these will do for spring spawning cat-fish. The closer to deep water the better and the earlier these areas will be used by catfish. If there is a steam plant, either nuclear, coal-fired or gas-fired, fishing where the warm water is dumped back out into the lake or river will make your season at least two weeks earlier. On places like Kentucky Lake, the timing is about the last week in April. Regardless of where you fish, you can figure on catfish starting to spawn when the water temperature hits the low sixties. They will continue to spawn as the weather warms until the spawn is over, which is typically around the last of June to the first of July.

Many anglers fish for spawning catfish on the riprap of dams and road causeways.

If you're looking for early fish, look for riprap with a southern exposure. Places on the north and northwest side of the lake get the most thermal energy from sun and warm quicker. It also helps if the riprap areas have some current. It doesn't have to be a strong river current; it can be either windblown or secondary current adjacent to deep water. The closer to deep water the easier it is for catfish to come up out of the river channel and locate on the rocks.

Using your depth finder, work one contour level at a time. If it's been fairly warm, go to five feet of water and work 100 or 150 yards laterally along the shore, fishing the same depth. If you don't get a bite, move to two or three feet, and then change to six feet, eight feet, ten feet—just keep changing the depth and working contour lines laterally until you find the depth they're located. It's basically just casting combined with slow trolling with your trolling motor. A good rig is a No. 4 to 6 treble hook for shad guts, nightcrawlers, or bait shrimp. A No. 6 circle hook works well for cut bait. Above the bait use split shot, then a three- or four-inch-long balsa wood or Styrofoam, cigar-shaped slip cork.

DRIFT FISHING

Truman Lake guide Jeff Faulkenberry of Endless Season Guide Service with a nice blue cat taken while drift fishing.

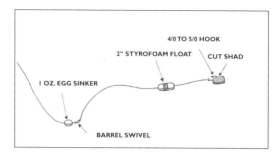

Rod and reel drift fishing is a favorite catfish tactic on some of the larger reservoirs. Special drift rigs, with Styrofoam floats, are used to hold cut shad or live baits just off the bottom. Using this rig and locating catfish-holding spots, or actually

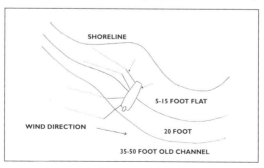

looking for fish with LCRs, anglers drift or slow troll with cut and live baits.

During the spring months flats next to deep water are best, while the "drops" or edges between deep and shallow water are best during the summer months. Depth will range from 12 to 60 feet deep. Following the depth contour with several lines out can result in some productive catfishing for big cats. Jeff Faulkenberry of Endless Season Guide Service on Truman Reservoir in central Missouri is a master at this technique. Jeff utilizes four rods in rod holders and uses cut shad almost exclusively. He basically uses a No. 8 circle hook on a 50-pound test shock leader. A three-way swivel is used to tie a Lindy Slinky weight, from 1-½ to 2 ounces, as well as the main 30-pound test line and the shock leader. Above the hook is a two-inch float. Although Jeff will anchor and fish if necessary, he prefers to drift across

Drift fishing utilizes rods in rod holders and drifting across likely catfish holding spots.

Various means are used to slow the drift in the wind including the old-fashioned sea anchor.

the flats, using his trolling motor only to maintain direction. He likes to drift at .5 to 1.5 miles per hour and has used drift socks to slow down speed. Now he uses Power Paddles, an electronic "anchor" to slow down the drift. Jeff has also experimented with an old walleye tactic, using planer boards to spread out his lines, with great results.

TAILRACE ANGLING

If there's one single fishing situation that provides the most opportunity for the most fishermen to tangle with big cats, it's the tailrace waters below the larger dams. From early spring throughout the summer months, these areas provide good catfishing, especially for the larger cats such as blues and flatheads. The big draw again is current. Usually the more current the better, except in the very early spring when there may be too much current for safe or even productive fishing. These areas can often be fished either from the bank or by boat. Both have their advantages and disadvantages. Bank fishermen are naturally restricted by the distance they can toss their baits into the water, and when fishing is really good there can be a fairly large crowd to fight. On the other hand, bank fishing is not quite as much work as boat fishing and a bit safer. It can still be dangerous, should you happen to fall into the churning, high current water or get caught in the wrong spot when the dam gates are opened.

One of the biggest problems of bank fishing is hangups. With all the current, riprap, and debris filling the tailrace area below most dams, you might as well buy interest in a tackle store, because you're going to lose a lot of hooks, bait, and sinkers.

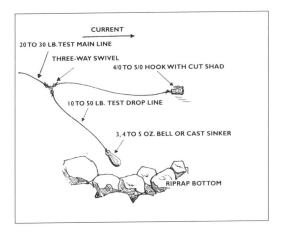

CURRENT

20 TO 30 LB. TEST MAIN LINE

THREE-WAY SWIVEL

4/0 TO 5/0 HOOK WITH CUT SHAD

10 TO 50 LB. TEST DROP LINE

3, 4 TO 5 OZ. BELL OR CAST SINKER

RIPRAP BOTTOM

Although standard, heavy-duty fishing gear can be used for this type of fishing, specialized rod outfits are used by many serious tailrace fishermen. These are usually big, 10- to 12-foot long surf rods fitted with heavy-duty, saltwater reels. Loaded with 30- to 40-pound test line and a 4-ounce or bigger sinker, they're a bit hard to use at first. The big rods are used primarily to add distance to the cast with the heavy rigs, enabling anglers to get out in the middle of the wide channels below many dams. It takes some practice, not to mention muscle, but the rods can toss baited hooks a great distance and the stiffness of the rods can be a big help when battling a 50-pound flathead or blue cat in fast current.

Most anglers tie a heavy, three-way swivel on the line, then a dropper line of the same weight to hold the hook. A second dropper line of lighter test is used to hold the weight. When the weight becomes snagged, and it will, you can often break the lighter line to prevent losing the entire rig. Some anglers, however, simply make a three-way tie in the line, eliminating the swivel.

Bait choice depends on what is the most prevalent bait in the area, with shad being the single best choice with many anglers, although goldfish and even prepared baits can be used.

The best time of the year for this action is early in the spring when cats are drawn up below the dams by flushing water and then in the fall and even through the winter months.

During the summer months when rivers get low, the water just below the dam often provides current to attract big cats, and jigging spoons, crankbaits, and jigs can be used to catch big flatheads.

Although many areas have "No Boating Zones" directly below the dam, some

Tailrace angling can also provide some giant cats.

don't, or the "No Boating Zone" may be quite small. Fishing the "boils" or the surging pockets of current directly below dams is a productive but extremely dangerous tactic. Again, special tactics and gear are used. It, of course, requires expert boating skills. Rods are usually stiff, sawn-off, solid fiberglass, rigged with a sturdy casting reel loaded with 45- to 100-pound test line. A ½- to 1-pound sinker is used to get the rig to the bottom in the fast current. One to three dropper hooks baited with cut shad are tied to the main line. Once the cat takes it, it's usually handlined or brought in by hand.

TROTLINING

Trotlining is one of the most interesting and productive methods of catching catfish. It's also one of the best tactics for catching the really big cats and, with a little work, you can fill a freezer quite economically.

Trotlining can be productive in streams and rivers, lakes, ponds, or reservoirs—actually any place there are catfish. About the only thing you'll need is a boat, and it certainly doesn't have to be an expensive one. The boat and motor can be anything that can safely be used on the water you will be fishing.

A trotline is basically a stout cord stretched through the water with baited hooks on droppers tied onto the cord. Trotlines can be purchased in almost

any tackle or bait store and through mail order catalogs.

Or you can make up your own quite easily. Length can run from 50 feet to 100 yards, depending on hooks used. (Note: Make sure you check local laws regarding trotlines. Most define the length allowed as well as number of hooks and hook spacing. In most instances trotlines must also be labeled with the owner's name and address.)

Trotlines can be made up varying from light to extra heavy, and most anglers

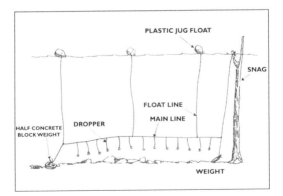

PLASTIC JUG FLOAT

SNAG

FLOAT LINE

MAIN LINE

DROPPER

HALF CONCRETE
BLOCK WEIGHT

WEIGHT

prefer to make them up fairly heavy. Use only good quality nylon cording for both the main staging and the droppers. Main lines are usually made of 300- to 600-pound test nylon while the droppers are No. 12 nylon line doubled and tied to create a dropper approximately 12 to 18 inches long. Nylon line can be either white or green. Trotlines are made up as fixed dropper, where the droppers are tied permanently to the line or you can use special metal clip fasteners that simply snap over the line and can be removed or snapped in place at will. You can also use large snap swivels. Once assembled, a permanent trotline is ready to use. The main disadvantage of the fixed or permanent trotline is it can be a nightmare of tangled hooks and lines unless you're extremely careful and like to spend a great deal of time putting in and taking out a trotline. Each hook has to be carefully attached to a holding board or reel as the line is brought in.

Regardless of type of trotline, the dropper lines should be attached to the main line with swivels. Catfish often escape a trotline by simply twisting the line until something gives, and swivels prevent this problem. Small metal swivel stops are available that can be crimped on the line or use split shot.

The strongest method of tying on the hooks is to push the dropper loop through the eye of the hook and then back over the hook. This also turns the hook around and into the fish.

Weights are used to hold the trotline down in the water, and the object used depends on the size of the trotline, depth, and so forth. There are several sources for weights, including old metal sash weights, heavy bricks or concrete blocks, as well as plastic jugs filled with sand or cement.

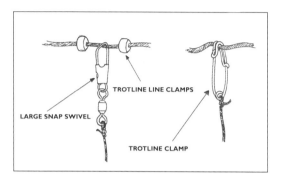

LARGE SNAP SWIVEL

TROTLINE LINE CLAMPS

TROTLINE CLAMP

Weight lines should be made somewhat longer than dropper lines.

Floats are required to mark the location of the line for boaters, skiers, and swimmers, and discarded plastic jugs or bottles are the most popular choice.

Hooks used these days are 3/0 to 5/0 and usually deep circle, which bend almost back on themselves and are hard for cats to escape.

Trotline Sets

There are as many different varieties of trotline sets as there are fishermen who use them, and with experience each fisherman will find a particular type of set that suits him. The sets must also be tailored to the particular water situation. For instance, trotlines set in the deep water channels of impounded lakes are quite different from the trotlines set below a riffle in a shallow, fast-moving stream, or one set in a cut bank or pocket of such a stream.

In any case, the main line is usually stretched across the area to be fished; it may be fairly short or several hundred feet long. The dropper lines are attached

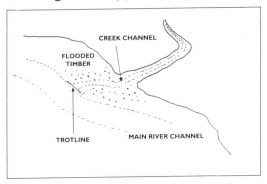

at regular intervals, the distance depending on the length and size of the set.
Trotliners after the big cats space their
drop lines five feet apart to prevent big
cats entangling their lines and getting
away.

The exact spot to set a trotline depends
on whether it is in a lake or stream. In
most instances cats will follow a definite
migration route in their foraging. In a
lake, this may be the old river channel.

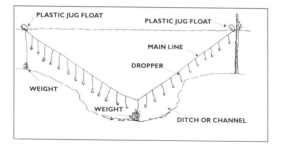

Lake sets are usually made by fastening
one end to a shoreline object or a stand-
ing submerged tree and using an anchor

for the other end. Sets can also be made
using two anchors.

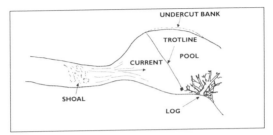

Best choices for stream sets are near
the deep undercut banks or bends that
lead up to a shoal. Upstream of log jams

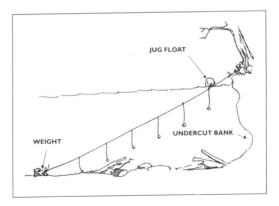

and brush piles or other good cover are also good places for a trotline.

In rivers, many trotliners like to make the set at an angle with the upper end fastened to a sturdy tree limb and the outer end held in place with a large anchor. The spaced hooks are then held at different depths down to the anchor.

Setting out a non-fixed line should be done in steps for ease and safety. Anchor the main line in place first, then starting at the solid end, bait the droppers and snap them in place working to the end or middle weights. Remove in the same manner.

Trotlining can be dangerous, and all boating safety precautions should be observed. If working a stream, always bait or work a trotline from the downstream side and wear a life preserver at all times. By the same token, you should have a good belt knife that can be grabbed quickly in an emergency. A heavy trotline in swift cur-

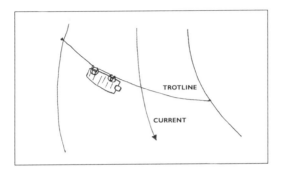

TROTLINE

CURRENT

rent can be mighty dangerous, and you can easily become entangled in the hooks and pulled underwater.

In most instances, it's easier and safer when two fishermen work the lines. One can hold the main line and pull the boat along the line while the other baits up, clips or unclips droppers in place, and lands fish.

LIMB-LINING

This is quite similar to trotlining, except individual lines are tied onto overhanging tree branches. This is primarily done in streams, and although channels, bullheads, and blues are caught, the primary

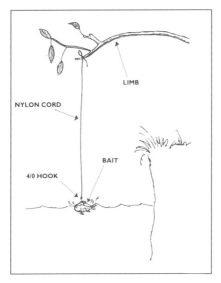

LIMB

NYLON CORD

BAIT

4/0 HOOK

objectives are the big flatheads. Although other cats will take almost anything from dead chicken guts to pieces of shrimp and will prowl the bottoms of the lakes and rivers looking for food, big flatheads will only take live bait and it's got to be plenty fresh and lively. They also tend to cover all depths in pursuit of food; therefore the best flathead limb line set consists of a line tied to a strong but whippy limb overhanging the bank of a river, large reservoir, or lake. A 4/0 to 5/0 hook is tied to the line and baited with either a black perch or big goldfish. The fish must be hooked just behind and below the dorsal fin.

Some anglers like to position the bait just below the surface of the water. In fact, many flathead hunters like to position the bait with the tip of the dorsal fin out of the water. The frantic circling action of the captive bait is like ringing a dinner bell to

any big flatheads in the area. The line is tied to a sturdy but flexible limb so big cats can't break it off.

Another tactic for limb lines is to submerge the bait with a heavy weight placed just above the hook and the bait suspended just off the bottom. This is especially effective for channels and blue cats.

Regardless of which method is used, or a combination of methods, it's best to put out several lines. Be sure to adhere to local rules and regulations.

JUGGING FOR CATS

One of the most popular tactics for catfishing is jug fishing.

Jugging is also a good tactic for catching a nice stringer of cats. It can be used almost anywhere there is a good catfish population, except in extremely swift current.

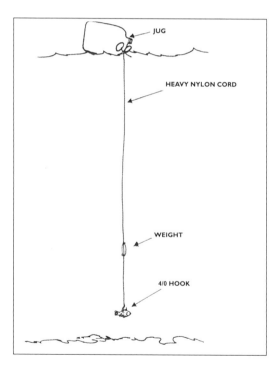

Then you'll spend more time chasing and unsnagging jugs than catching fish.

Done correctly, jugging is probably the simplest and easiest kind of fishing possible. Merely tie a line to a plastic jug, tie on a weight and a hook, bait it up and throw it in the water. Then sit back and watch for the action. Varying the line depth on the jugs determines the best depths for catching cats. Some prefer anchored jugs, using heavy weights to hold individual jugs in place, often leaving them overnight and checking first thing in the morning. These days "noodle" jugs, either purchased or homemade, are often used instead of the old-time plastic jug.

If you're fishing an area that has current or wind to move the jugs, it's a matter of following the drifting jugs with a boat, unsnagging those that snag up, taking cats off the hooks, and rebaiting.

Jug fishing is an excellent method of fishing small lakes or ponds. Tie on the main

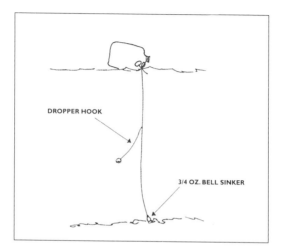

DROPPER HOOK

3/4 OZ. BELL SINKER

line for different depths, tie a weight on the end of the line, add dropper hooks, and toss out.

The jug will drift until the weight hits the bottom then stop, the dropper hooks floating just above the bottom. With lines of different depths set out, the jugs will simply float around the pond until all the weights are resting on the bottom. The variety of bottom depths regulates the locations of the jugs. These days there are also lighted jugs that signal a strike.

The expectation of watching a handful of jugs, waiting for the fish to bite, is akin to fishing with a bobber, with the jugs as giant "bobbers." When one starts dancing and moving through the water, you know you have a cat. What kind and how big will it be—you just never know!

GETTING AND KEEPING LIVE BAITS

A wide variety of baits are available for catfish, including prepared baits, homemade concoctions, and live bait.

A variety of bait-gathering products are available.

Although a lot of catfish baits are "stink" baits, the best choice for many cats is live bait, including earthworms, nightcrawlers, crawfish, and a variety of baitfishes, including minnows, shiners, goldfish, shad, skip-jack herring, carp, buffalo, suckers, and perch. If you want to use live bait for catfish, having the bait you need at the right time is an important facet of live bait catfish angling, and keeping bait can be even more invaluable.

Worms

Probably the single most popular, easy to obtain and use catfish bait is a glob of worms. This can be the ordinary garden variety, huge river worms, manure worms, or nightcrawlers. For catfishing, the bigger the better, not only in size, but amount as well. You'll need a good supply of worms to catfish. Nightcrawlers are available almost anywhere, including many quick-stop stations, even in grocery stores in some locales. But there are crawlers and there are *crawlers*. The best crawlers are fat and sassy.

You can also collect your own earthworms, river worms, and crawlers. Digging in your backyard or garden may produce plenty of wigglers for your catfishing foray. Finding the right spot to dig for them, however, is extremely important. Worms prefer damp areas with rich soil, such as along creek and river banks, around drain openings, and around the edges of barnyards. Look under boards and other debris to find moister areas. Leaf mulch also provides an excellent earthworm source. River worms are found along the wet riverbanks and are longer versions of earthworms.

Nightcrawlers can also be collected. The best time is after a long, soaking nighttime rain. As the rain saturates the soil, it drives the crawlers up to the surface. Best places to prospect for them are on closely mowed lawns and on fairly cool, moist evenings in the summertime. They're easy to spook, however, and you can also easily break them if you try to pull them from their holes. You can oftentimes simply pick a good number off your driveway, on the sidewalks, and I sometimes even find them in my garage. If the rain stops in the night, you can quite often collect nightcrawlers with a flashlight with a red lens in short-cropped grass areas. Folks have invented many different tactics and products for collecting worms. Some utilize a battery-powered unit that stimulates worms and drives them to the surface. One old-fashioned method is "fiddling up" worms. A notched stick is driven into the ground and another stick rubbed up and down the notches to create a vibration to bring worms to the surface. A potato fork driven into the ground and struck with another object also sometimes works.

Keeping earthworms is fairly easy and growing a supply is also fairly easy. Growing nightcrawlers takes a bit more effort, but keeping them is again fairly easy. Simply keep them in a Styrofoam box in a refrigerator. You can keep a good quantity in this manner, and when you head to the lake simply take a small Styrofoam cooler with a day's supply. A small ice pack in the cooler will help keep the worms throughout the day, especially if the day is hot. Some anglers like to condition their worms the night before by placing them between ice-cold layers of wet newspaper, or you can simply toss them in a container of ice water the night before. They will be fat and wiggly.

You can easily raise garden worms, or purchased "red wigglers," but raising nightcrawlers takes a great deal more expertise and work. You'll need a container to hold the worms—a large old cooler is a good choice—but you must drill a few small holes in the top for ventilation. Fill the container with good garden soil that is not sandy. Thoroughly mix in one cup of dry dog food and sprinkle about a quart of water over the soil. Place twenty-five to fifty earthworms on top of the soil. Dampen a couple of sheets of newspaper and place over the worms.

Place the worm box in a cool part of your basement, away from the furnace, but where the temperature will stay 60 to 75 degrees Fahrenheit. Temperature is very important. If the temperature rises much above 70 degrees, the worms may die; if the temperature drops below 60 degrees, reproduction may be slowed. Use an inexpensive thermometer to monitor the soil temperature.

Inspect your worm box once a week. If the surface is dry, add a little water, but don't overwater. If the soil is muddy, you're overfeeding and overwatering. About every three weeks remove the top two or three inches of soil and mix in one-half cup of dry dog food. Dump the remainder of the soil out and check on your worm "herd." Place the newly fed soil in the bottom of the container and replace the rest of the soil and the worms. In six to eight weeks you should have a new crop of worms. And if you're a good worm farmer, you can expect from 700 to 1,000 worms.

Earthworms and nightcrawlers can be kept using a variety of products available.

Raising nightcrawlers, however, is a bit trickier. They require a bedding temperature of 40 to 50 degrees Fahrenheit. You can keep a large supply, however, over a long period of time if you have a refrigerator and a worm box that fits inside it. Quite frankly, if you're going to try raising nightcrawlers, your best bet is the Magic Products worm bedding.

Worms are used on single point rather than treble hooks. When rod and reel fishing for channels, the hook size is usually 2/0 to 3/0. When trotlining, using set lines, and when fishing water with big cats, the hook size is often 4/0 to even 5/0.

The procedure is simple—several earthworms are threaded onto the hook to produce a big glob of the wiggling creatures. Worms will catch all species of cats.

Crawfish

Crawfish, or crawdads as they are often called, are also excellent catfish bait. They are particularly good when placed on set lines or trotlines for "big" cats such as blues, channels, and flatheads. The alternative is bait shrimp sold in bait shops, but it's softer and often doesn't stay on the hook as well.

Crawdads can be purchased at most bait shops; however, half the fun of using them is catching them, and the most productive method is seining with a minnow

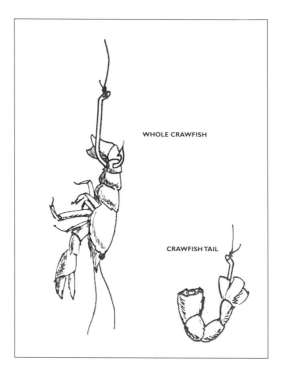

WHOLE CRAWFISH

CRAWFISH TAIL

seine. Crawdads can be found in almost any small, shallow stream, particularly if it is clear. They can be found in ponds as well.

Minnows, crawfish, and other live baits can often by trapped with a minnow trap.

Crawfish can also be trapped using small minnow traps. Add a bit of meat or chunk of old bread to the trap and set it in the slow-moving portion of a stream. You can also bait the trap with canned cat food. Just punch holes in the cat food can and put the whole can in the trap. Check it about once a day, and you'll eventually end up with a bucket of crawfish.

The hardest part of fishing with crawfish is keeping them. If you're going to be using

Purchased aerating systems can also be used for home storage of baits.

them right away, an insulated foam minnow bucket can be used to transport them, but make sure the lid is kept on because they can climb right up the sides of the bucket. To keep over longer periods, a large tub partially filled with water with a rock in the center for them to crawl out on will suffice. Or use an aerated bait tank with a cage partially suspended above water so they can occasionally crawl out in the air.

A minnow trap works well for this. Make sure you freshen the water several times a day and add ice cubes to keep the water cool or use an aerator to provide oxygen.

One of the most successful methods is keeping crawfish in a wooden live box with screened sides. Keep this in a stream or pond and feed the crawfish a diet of meat or dead fish.

Two basic methods are used for hooking crawfish. The first is to merely fasten them on the hook through the back of the tail. This is primarily used on set lines because crawfish on rod and reel lines will often manage to crawl back under rocks, logs, and so forth. Some expert catfishermen prefer to remove the pinchers before fastening on the hook.

The second method is to peel the meat out of the tail and thread it onto the hook in the manner of cut bait. This can be an extremely effective catfish bait although some fishermen use bait shrimp available at bait shops or grocery stores in lieu of the latter method.

Other Live Baits

Any number of forage fish will attract catfish, including non-game and some game fish. Make sure you understand state laws regarding the use of forage fish as bait. Big chub minnows, goldfish, bluegill, and perch are all good choices.

Live bait is the best choice for many areas, especially when targeting blues and channel cats.

Where legal, bluegill are an extremely productive bait for flatheads.

Frogs and insects of all kinds can also be used as catfish bait. Leeches can be purchased at bait shops or gathered from small streams with traps baited with bloody meat.

Cut Bait

All of these baits can be used in a variety of techniques for the various catfish species. You may, however, be limited to what you can purchase in your local area. You

Cut bait is often the choice when targeting blues.

can also use a minnow trap or even a seine to acquire some of the smaller baitfish, including bluegills and sunperch (where legal to use). A tiny Tru-Turn hook, split shot, and bobber can be used to acquire perch, and this in itself is a lot of fun.

Herring and shad are another matter. Although these are usually used as cut bait, and often available frozen at bait shops, fresh bait makes the best cut bait. Live fresh bait is often another choice, but it's harder to keep some of these species alive, even while fishing, especially shad. Two species of shad are found in most river systems and larger reservoirs. Gizzard shad grow the largest, often to a foot in length and are the hardiest. Shad can be used in various ways; however, in most instances it's used as cut bait, because shad are so hard to keep alive. That doesn't matter, because shad cut bait is just as good as fresh shad for catfish.

Cut shad is used on trotlines, set lines, for rod and reel fishing, and drift fishing, and it is extremely popular as a bait for fishing the tailrace water below dams. This is because enormous amounts of shad come through the turbines of the dam wounded or minced into little pieces. Large numbers of catfish collect below the dams at certain times of year to gorge on the feast. Shad is a good bait for blues and channels alike.

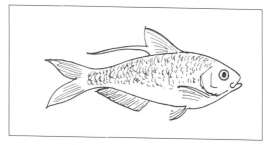

Although some bait shops sell fresh shad, they charge extremely high prices because of the cost of keeping them. Many shops sell frozen shad, which works quite well for the price.

Any area where you plan to use shad for bait, however, will have a plentiful supply on hand for anyone wishing to collect them. Two basic methods are used. The first is to use an ultralight rod equipped with tiny treble hooks and "snag" or grab the shad as they swirl in schools below the dam. (This may be illegal in some states, so check with local game and fish laws.) A faster method for collecting larger amounts is to use a cast net. This is simply a large circular, weighted net that is cast out, over the water, allowed to fall down over the fish, then pulled up to capture the schooling shad. Cast nets are available in several sizes. Make sure you use a size that is legal in your state. Keep the net in a plastic bucket during storage, and keep it clean of debris. With a little practice, almost anyone can learn to use these fun bait catchers.

First step is to locate shad. They feed on algae, so look for them in shallow bays, around marinas, docks, and riprap where algae grows. And you'll usually have to work to locate and catch them. A good sonar unit can reveal schooling shad, making the chore somewhat easier.

Throwing a cast net is not particularly easy, and it does take some practice. Following are the steps for a right-handed person.

Shad and other baitfish can be gathered using a cast net.

1. Tie the rope around your right wrist and coil the rope into your throwing hand.

2. Hold the net by your side, resting the weights on the ground or boat deck. Grasp the net with your throwing hand at pocket height.

3. Grasp the lead line with your free hand at a position straight down from the end of your right thumb and place between thumb and forefinger.

4. Grasp the lead line with your free hand at a position about one arm's length from your other hand. This will hold the net one-quarter open.

5. Rotate your body back to the right a quarter turn and immediately rotate back to your left, releasing the net at a slight upward angle into the air in the direction of your target.

6. The net should hit the water in a circular form. Let the net sink to the desired depth and pull on the throw line to close the net. Grasp the horn of the net and release the throw line to empty the net into a bucket or bait well.

You can keep shad for live use in a good aeration system tank, but it's difficult and you'll lose many of them. Shad to be used for cut bait should be placed on ice with ice over them. You really can't keep shad much longer than 24 hours in most instances. It's best to freeze shad left over from the day, but frozen shad do tend to become soft. To freeze, place them in a saltwater brine, and freeze in bags with the brine solution.

Regardless of how you get them, bait-fish left at the end of the day can present a problem. As mentioned, shad don't last long; perch and other baitfish, however, can be kept in a good aerated tank system for longer. Many products are now available, including tanks, aerators, and water treatment chemicals that aid in keeping baitfish frisky and healthy. You can keep a limited number alive with a DC- or battery-powered aerator, and some aerator units can be placed in any container. A big insulated cooler makes a good bait-

An aerated bait tank can be used to hold any number of live baits. The tank shown utilizes 110V-aerator with a plastic stock tank.

fish tank. A 110V-system can also be set up to keep bait indefinitely. A number of aerators for use in tanks are available, as are tanks and/or complete units. The electric supply must be protected by a ground–fault interrupter.

My system consists of a Rubbermaid 60-gallon stock tank with a 110V-aerator. This is quite a simple system, but it can also be improved with a bit of effort. In order to support the agitator and also to keep the bait quiet and prevent algae growth from light, make a lid of ⅜-inch treated plywood, with a hinged lift-up section. Actually the lid is in three sections, and I divided the tank in half to keep a variety of baitfish. A piece of treated plywood with a center hole cut out and galvanized screen wire fastened over the hole is the divider. It's fastened to a cleat on the underside of the center top piece, which is anchored solidly to the tank top. Lids on both sides are hinged to the center strip. This works quite well, but you can improve the keeping ability by adding an overflow drain tube and an intake attached to a garden hose. It doesn't take much; just a trickle of fresh water will maintain livelier bait. The tank should be placed in a cool dark spot in your garage or shed.

Several tactics can also help keep baits longer. First, remove all dead bait immediately. Check your tank morning and evening and remove any dead fish. Limit handling of all bait as much as possible, and then handle them gently. Rock salt (approximately 1-½ cups per 26 gallons) can be added each time you fill the tank to help keep scales intact. Rinse agitator and tank thoroughly after each use to reduce harmful bacteria and algae. Baitfish can be transported in minnow buckets, aerated minnow buckets, or live wells. Aerated minnow buckets are the best choice.

A variety of minnow buckets are available for holding baits while fishing.

Shad can be used whole, although a better method is to cut off side fillets. Some anglers prefer to use the head, cutting it off just behind the gills. The latter is the best choice when small fish are nibbling away at your bait. Jeff Faulkenberry likes to cut off the tail of whole shad so they'll release more blood, while big shad are cut into smaller sections. Shad guts, or the intestines from gizzard shad, are extremely popular with some southern anglers. There's a little knot on the top of the intestines that gives the shad its name. Take that, put it on the point of a hook, and it holds the rest of the guts in place.

TRADITIONAL STINK BAITS

Liver

Liver is an all-time favorite catfish food for most catfish species according to many studies, as well as the lore of old-time cat-fishermen. In fact, you just about can't go wrong threading a piece of chicken liver on a treble hook and throwing it into a known channel cat hole.

Liver, however, is smelly, messy, and hard to get—and keep—on the hook. Chicken liver quickly dissolves from the action of the water, gets thrown off the hook in an over-exuberant toss, or is quickly nibbled away by small fish. Other types of liver, including calf's liver, pork liver, and even deer liver, will also work, but are not quite as productive.

Stink Baits

Here's where we really get into the good stuff. Most successful prepared baits smell bad enough to rot the socks off a railyard bum, and a day spent catfishing with them will almost guarantee a night alone. There are probably more recipes for catfish bait, including homemade brews as well as commercially prepared baits, than you can imagine, and most expert brewers keep their secret ingredients close to their hearts. The main ingredients can vary, but most include these items:

Blood Baits—One of the most popular types of prepared baits are the blood baits. Chicken or slaughterhouse blood is allowed to coagulate by pouring it out onto a porous item, such as an old burlap sack, then cutting it into chunks and threading onto a hook. The biggest problem is that it eventually dissolves and won't stay in place. Mixing cotton in with the blood before it dries helps a great deal. Or you can use small sponge rubber balls on treble hooks. Dip in the blood bait and allow to dry for a blood doughball.

Meat Baits—Along the same line of the blood baits are pieces of half-rotten meat. A favorite of many catfishermen is a half-rotten rabbit or chicken carcass. Either will take some really huge river cats. Chicken guts were, in fact, a favorite bait of an uncle of mine. Living on a farm, there was quite often an old hen or two that succumbed to the heat or varmints, as well as plenty of chicken guts left from dressing frying chickens, and all went into a gunny sack hanging in the sun on a pole behind the barn. When this was "ripe" enough to suit, my uncle would haul the sack down to the river, tie a rock to it and drop the weighted sack in a favorite fishing hole. He would usually wait over-night, then the following morning would head to the river with some chicken livers or prepared blood baits.

Prepared Baits

Prepared baits are available in doughball form, squeeze tube, or dip bait. These days there are a number of extremely effective and productive no-mess cat-fishing systems that even the finickiest

Prepared paste and dip baits are readily available and easy to use.

angler can use. The dip baits utilize a sponge-covered hook which is dipped and swirled around in a thin bait the consistency of thick cream. The tubes are used with hollow plastic bait holders that are filled with bait squeezed from the tube. The latter are quick and easy even for beginners and children to use, and there is very little mess. Hollow tubes to hold bait are available in several

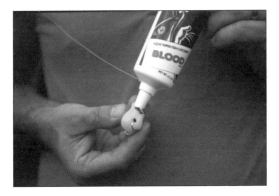

Paste-type baits can be squeezed into hollow tube lures for ease of use.

sizes and shapes, including crawfish. In a pinch you can use a tube Gitzit bass lure.

Doughball or dough baits must be of the right consistency to be productive. Too hard and they can't be molded on the hook; too soft, on the other hand, and it won't stay on the hook. If the bait is too hard, warm in the sunlight or add cooking oil or water and stir. If too soft, add flour, allow to cool, or form on the hook, then hold under cold water to allow to cool and firm.

Dip baits must also be of the proper consistency, and again, they can be warmed or cooled or mixed with warm water or flour to change the consistency. To use, they are first stirred for 30 seconds or so, then a dip rig is dipped into them and stirred around with a small stick or paddle. Make sure the rig is thoroughly saturated and covered.

Making Your Own Dip Rig

You can purchase the dip rigs or make up your own as shown by using pieces of old plastic worms, rubber bands, and treble hooks.

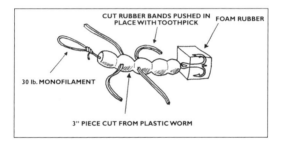

CUT RUBBER BANDS PUSHED IN PLACE WITH TOOTHPICK

FOAM RUBBER

30 lb. MONOFILAMENT

3" PIECE CUT FROM PLASTIC WORM

You can also make up your own prepared baits, including dough baits. They are made by mixing water and flour to form into balls. Then boil briefly to give them firmness. Blood, cheese paste, or decomposed fish can be added to the mixture. Or you can make the dough-balls ahead of time and soak in the flavorings.

Cheese doughballs are a popular favorite and are fairly easy to make. The main ingredient is a rancid, strong smelling cheese. Mix with bread as a stiffener or add in small pieces of cotton to make a tougher cheese doughball.

Regardless of the basic flavoring of the doughballs, many anglers also like to add a bit of anise oil.

HOMEMADE DIP BAIT

Making your own dip bait is easy, if you can stand the smell. Here are the ingredients:

2 gallons minnows or shad
7 pounds limburger cheese
1 ounce oil of anise

Now comes the fun part. Place the minnows or shad in a bucket and add just enough water to cover. Place the bucket in the sun (protected from neighborhood cats) for several days until they get "ripe." Another tactic is to punch holes in the bottom of a bucket, place the minnows or shad in this, and bury for about a week.

In either case, once the mixture has become "ripe," remove, pour off the liquid, and mix the semi-liquid parts with the limburger cheese. Add the anise oil and blend all ingredients in an OLD blender, or simply mash and stir until a fine paste forms.

Pour this mixture into old fruit jars, or better yet, used plastic food containers. Fill only half full and don't tighten lids down. The mixture should be left to ferment for a further week or two and can more than double in volume. The result is a soft dip bait about the consistency of butter. To use, dip the rig into the bait and stir around with a stick. The baits will last longer if kept refrigerated in an OLD refrigerator.

Other Baits

Some fairly unusual baits can be used for catching cats. Plain old Ivory soap is a popular choice with some anglers, and persimmons are a favorite fall bait. Freshwater clams or mussels that have been chopped up and soaked in milk in the sun until they have spoiled is also a favorite, particularly with commercial fishermen on the Mississippi River.

Chumming for Cats

Regardless of whether you're fishing from the bank or a boat, chumming or baiting a hole is an excellent tactic for bringing in numbers of catfish. You don't have to search for the cats, they'll find you. (Make sure you check local laws regarding baiting.)

You can purchase manufactured products for baiting a catfish hole, but you can easily make up your own. The ingredients are maize or milo (available at feed and grain stores) and water. Place the grain in a plastic bucket, cover with water, add a lid, and allow to set in the sun until it ferments. This will usually take about three to four days.

To use, place the grain in a burlap sack along with a rock, tie to a strong line, and drop in the area you wish to bait. You can mark the location with an old plastic jug for future reference. The best tactic, however, is to simply fling the soured grain out over the area you intend to fish. It won't take long before old Mr. Whiskers shows up.

If the fish are located in shallow water, position the boat a short distance away from the baited area and cast into it. Baits to use include prepared dough baits, earthworms, and so forth.

It's a good idea to put out several such holes. Fish one until the cats get a bit wary, then simply move to your next honey hole.

Locating catfish in streams depends primarily on the species.

Blues love the current pockets just below the dams, or on the outer edge of a wing dam.

Channels like to lie near these pockets or in holding spots near them. Brushpiles and log jams are excellent prospecting spots for channels, particularly if they are just below a shoal or shallow.

Flatheads, like most predatory species, are primarily lazy. They'll hold in any pocket that will sweep baitfish into them. They tend to lie up in dark holes, such as under bluffs, rock cover, and so forth, during the daylight and come out to prowl at night.

In lakes, look for all species of cats near a migratory route such as an old river channel. Channels will more often venture into the shallows throughout the year and can even be caught from the banks, especially during early spring. Flatheads can also be caught shallow on lakes during the night hours. Blues will be found in the deeper channels or those having even the slightest current. In fact, a good tactic of catching blues is to structure fish just as in bass fishing, looking for the breaks and migratory routes between shallow and deep water. Bullheads can be found in the backs of the coves or any place with warm shallow water.

ABOUT THE AUTHOR

Monte Burch is a confessed all-out cat-fishing addict. Regardless of type—channel cats in ponds and lakes, blues from the tailrace waters, or flatheads off traditional limb lines—he grew up catfishing—and still is.

He combines in this book many of his childhood memories and tactics passed down from generations with modern tactics and products for the best in catfishing, regardless of the species or location.

Monte is a regular contributor to many outdoor magazines and the author of numerous books on the outdoors, do-it-yourself projects, and rural living.

NOTES

NOTES